Beginner Belgium Cookbook

Deliciously Easy Belgium Recipes for the Whole Family

BY - Stephanie Sharp

wwwwwwwwwwwwwwwwwwwwwwwwwwwwwwwwwwwww

License Notes

WWWWWWWWWWWWWWWWWWWWWWWWWWWWWWWWWWWWW

Table of Contents

Introduction

Belgium boasts the most three-star restaurants than any other nation per capita, including France. Belgium is known for its great cooks. The home cooks spend time thinking about what they are going to cook, shopping for, discussing, preparing and celebrating food.

Belgium's French foundation, heartily influenced by Germany and Holland, herbs directly from a Medieval garden, and spices and condiments from an elaborate Flemish culture, Belgium have an interesting cuisine - sophisticated comfort food -- slow-cooked, bourgeois, honest, nostalgic. To a Winter's day, it is the perfect antidote family picnics, continental dinner party and a great Sunday meal.

Peach Waffles

This recipe is delicious in the summertime when peaches are in season and full of flavor.

Serves: 7

Time: 20 minutes

Ingredients

- 2 cups white flour
- 1 tbsp granulated sugar
- 1 tsp cinnamon
- ¼ tsp 1 pinch nutmeg
- 1 1/3 tbsp baking powder
- 1 pinch sea salt
- 2 large eggs, room temperature
- 1 peach, sliced
- 1 cup whole milk
- ½ cup oil (canola)
- 1 tsp vanilla

Directions

1. Whisk together the eggs, whole milk, oil and vanilla extract. Combine your ingredients and break up the eggs.

2. Fold in the sliced peaches, covering the slices in the batter.

3. Add in your dry ingredients to the bowl, whisking constantly to ensure no lumps form in the batter.

4. Stir until a smooth batter forms then let the batter rest for 10 minutes, allowing the batter to thicken.

5. Set your waffle iron to preheat according to the manufacturer's directions. Once the iron is hot, spray with baking spray if needed then pour the waffle batter into the waffle maker.

6. Cook according to the manufacturer's directions then serve while hot.

7. Cook the remaining waffle batter using the same directions.

Asparagus with Eggs

Treat someone special to a lovely breakfast of Asparagus with Eggs using this recipe.

Serves: 6

Time: 20 minutes

Ingredients

- 3 lbs. of white asparagus with skin removed
- 3 warm hard boiled eggs
- 1 teaspoon of lemon juice
- 1 tablespoon of melted butter
- 7 tablespoons of butter
- chopped parsley, to garnish
- salt, to taste
- black pepper, to taste
- 1 pinch nutmeg

Directions:

1. Put the asparagus in salted boiling water. Cover, then cook on low heat for 30 minutes - until they are tender. Drain the asparagus.

2. Using a fork, mix the eggs with the butter, lemon juice and parsley. Add some salt, 1 pinch nutmeg and pepper.

3. Put the asparagus on plates and pour some of the sauce on top.

Sweet Potato Waffles

While these are a great side dish to a dinner or lunch, they are especially good with maple syrup as a savory and sweet breakfast.

Serves: 8

Time: 20 minutes

Ingredients

- 2 cups white flour
- 1 tbsp granulated sugar
- 1 tsp cinnamon
- ¼ tsp 1 pinch nutmeg
- 1 1/3 tbsp baking powder
- 1 pinch sea salt
- 1 large egg, room temperature
- 1 cup shredded sweet potato
- 1 ¼ cup whole milk
- ½ cup oil (canola, vegetable or coconut oil)
- 1 tsp vanilla

Directions

1. Whisk together the eggs, whole milk, oil and vanilla extract.

2. Combine all your ingredients and break up the eggs.

3. Stir in the shredded sweet potatoes.

4. Add in all your dry ingredients to the bowl, whisking constantly to ensure no lumps form in the batter.

5. Stir until a smooth batter forms then let the batter rest for 10 minutes, allowing the batter to thicken.

6. Set your waffle iron to preheat. Once the iron is hot, spray with baking spray if needed then pour the waffle batter into the waffle maker.

7. Cook according to the manufacturer's directions then serve hot.

8. Cook the remaining waffle batter using the same directions.

Leek Soup

For a nice warm bowl of rich, creamy comfort; try this bowl of Leek soup.

Serves: 4

Time: 3 hours 15 minutes

Ingredients

- 3 leeks with tops cut off and chopped
- 2 peeled and sliced onion
- 2 peeled and chopped potatoes
- ¼ tsp. black pepper
- ¼ tsp. salt
- 1oz. butter

Directions

1. Fry the onions in a little butter in saucepan for 8 minutes.

2. Add the leeks and potatoes with some salt and black pepper and fry for a further 8 minutes. Add enough water to cover the vegetables.

3. Cook on a low heat for 3 hours. Blend gently or pass the mix through a sieve.

Flemish Carrots

This is a nutrient packed family favorite. A great way to enjoy carrots.

Serves: 3

Time: 10 minutes

Ingredients

- 6 peeled and chopped carrots
- half pint/240ml of cream
- parsley (chopped for serving)
- ¼ tsp. sugar
- pinch of salt
- pinch of pepper

Directions

1. Put the carrots in a pan of boiling water. Cook on a low heat for 10 minutes - until cooked.

2. Drain the carrots.

3. Put the carrots back in the pan and add salt and pepper. Put back on a low heat, add the cream, and a quarter of a teaspoon of sugar then cook on a low heat for 5 minutes.

4. Add some chopped parsley and serve.

Apple Cider Waffles

Apple cider waffles are perfectly sweetened and just slightly tangy thanks to the tasty of the cider.

Serves: 6

Time: 15 minutes

Ingredients

- 2 cups white flour
- 1 tbsp granulated sugar
- 1 tsp ground cinnamon
- 1 1/3 tbsp baking powder
- 1 pinch sea salt
- 2 large eggs, room temperature
- ¾ cups whole milk
- 1 cup apple cider
- ½ cup oil (canola, vegetable or coconut oil)
- 1 tsp vanilla
- ¼ cup sugar
- 1 tsp ground cinnamon

Directions

1. Combine the ¼ cup sugar and 1 tsp ground cinnamon and stir together. Set aside.

2. Whisk together the eggs, whole milk, apple cider, oil and vanilla extract.

3. Combine all your ingredients and break up the eggs.

4. Add all of the dry ingredients, using just the 1 tbsp sugar and 1 tsp of the cinnamon, to the bowl, whisking constantly to ensure no lumps form in the batter.

5. Stir until a smooth batter forms then let the batter rest for 10 minutes, allowing the batter to thicken.

6. Set your waffle iron to preheat Once the iron is hot, spray with baking spray if needed then pour the waffle batter into the waffle maker.

7. Cook until golden then toss in the cinnamon sugar mix while they are hot.

8. Serve while hot and cook the remaining waffle batter using the same directions.

Red Cabbage and Apple Salad

This delicious Cabbage and Apple Salad is the perfect side for any entrée.

Serves: 4

Time: 7 hours 10 minutes

Ingredients

- 1 lb. of chopped red cabbage
- 1 apple peeled and sliced
- 1 cup of cider vinegar
- 1 ½ tbsp. of sugar
- half a cup of vegetable oil
- 1 bay leaf
- 1 sprig of thyme
- pinch of salt
- pinch of black pepper

Directions

1. Put the vinegar, bay leaf, thyme and sugar in a pan.

2. Cook on medium flame, stir constantly until the sugar has dissolved.

3. Put the salad in a bowl and pour over the vinegar while it is still warm. Leave to cool in a refrigerator for 7 hours.

4. Add the oil to the cabbage and toss. Discard the thyme and bay leaf.

5. Add the apple before serving.

Light Lemon Waffles

The delicate lemon taste of these waffles is a great way to brighten your morning.

Serves: 6

Time: 15 minutes

Ingredients

- 2 cups white flour
- 1 tbsp granulated sugar
- 1 tbsp fresh grated lemon zest
- 1 1/3 tbsp baking powder
- 1 pinch sea salt
- 2 large eggs, room temperature
- 1 ¾ cups whole milk
- ½ cup oil (canola, vegetable or coconut oil)
- 1 tsp vanilla
- ½ cup lemon curd

Directions

1. Whisk together the eggs, whole milk, lemon zest, oil and vanilla extract. Combine all your ingredients and break up the eggs.

2. Add in all your dry ingredients to the bowl, whisking constantly to ensure no lumps form in the batter.

3. Stir until a smooth batter forms then let the batter rest for 10 minutes, allowing the batter to thicken.

4. Set your waffle iron to preheat. Once the iron is hot, spray with baking spray if needed then pour the waffle batter into the waffle maker.

5. Cook until golden then serve while hot, topped with the lemon curd.

6. Cook the remaining waffle batter using the same directions. Serve.

Funfetti Waffles

The rainbow sprinkles in these waffles make the breakfast treat perfect for any celebration.

Serves: 6

Time: 15 minutes

Ingredients

- 2 cups white flour
- 1 tbsp granulated sugar
- 1 1/3 tbsp baking powder
- 1 pinch sea salt
- 2 large eggs, room temperature
- 1 ¾ cups whole milk
- ½ cup oil (canola, vegetable or coconut oil)
- 1 tsp vanilla
- ½ cup rainbow sprinkles

Directions

1. Whisk together the eggs, whole milk, oil and vanilla extract. Combine your ingredients and break up the eggs.

2. Add in your dry ingredients to the bowl, whisking constantly to ensure no lumps form in the batter. Stir until a smooth batter forms then let the batter rest for 10 minutes, allowing the batter to thicken.

3. Stir in the sprinkles gently, being careful not to over mix.

4. Set your waffle maker to preheat according to the manufacturer's directions.

5. Once the iron is hot, spray with baking spray if needed then pour the waffle batter into the waffle maker.

6. Cook until golden brown then serve while hot.

7. Cook the remaining waffle batter using the same directions.

Cinnamon Turnips

This tasty Cinnamon Turnip dish is simple to make and super delicious.

Serves: 4

Time: 7 hours 10 minutes

Ingredients

- 1 lb. of turnip peeled and cut into chunks
- parsley
- half teaspoon of cinnamon
- 3 tablespoons of butter
- Salt, to taste
- black pepper, to taste

Directions

1. Put the turnips in a saucepan. Cover with cold salted water and put on a lid. Boil, then cook on a low heat for 15 minutes.

2. Drain the turnips.

3. Put the butter in a pan and melt on a medium heat. Put the turnips in the pan along with the cinnamon, pepper and salt.

4. Cook for 10 minutes stirring the turnips around. Add some chopped parsley before serving.

Pumpkin Chocolate Chip Waffles

The rich chocolate chips pair so well with the pumpkin spices that you will definitely need to eat more than one.

Serves: 8

Time: 15 minutes

Ingredients

- 2 cups white flour
- 1 tbsp granulated sugar
- 1 tbsp pumpkin pie spice
- 1 1/3 tbsp baking powder
- 1 pinch sea salt
- 1 large eggs, room temperature
- ¼ cup pumpkin puree
- 1 ¾ cups whole milk
- ½ cup oil (canola, vegetable or coconut oil)
- 1 tsp vanilla
- ½ cup mini chocolate chips

Directions

1. Whisk together the eggs, pumpkin puree, whole milk, oil and vanilla extract. Combine your ingredients and break up the eggs.

2. Add in your dry ingredients to the bowl, whisking constantly to ensure no lumps form in the batter.

3. Stir until a smooth batter forms then let the batter rest for 10 minutes, allowing the batter to thicken.

4. Gently stir in the chocolate chips.

5. Set your waffle maker to preheat according to the manufacturer's directions. Once the iron is hot, spray with baking spray if needed then pour the waffle batter into the waffle maker.

6. Cook until golden brown then serve while hot.

7. Cook the remaining waffle batter using the same directions.

Liège Salad

This Belgium salad is extremely simple to whip up and is super delish.

Serves: 4

Time: 7 hours 10 minutes

Ingredients

- 17ozs of French green beans
- 2 oz of peeled and sliced potatoes
- 7 oz of chopped bacon
- 2 peeled and chopped onions
- 2 tablespoons of butter
- Vinegar, as needed
- Salt, to taste
- black pepper, to taste

Directions

1. Set your green beans to cook in boiling water for 4 minutes.

2. Drain.

3. Boil the potatoes in boiling water for 10 minutes - until cooked. Drain.

4. Set your onions in hot butter to fry in a pan. Add the bacon, bean and potatoes, cook on a medium heat for 5 minutes.

5. Add a little vinegar and some salt and pepper before serving.

Bacon and Beer Waffles

Bacon and beer come together in waffles that are a perfect snack for any time of year.

Serves: 7

Time: 15 minutes

Ingredients

- 2 cups white flour
- 1 tbsp granulated sugar
- 1 1/3 tbsp baking powder
- 1 pinch sea salt
- 2 large eggs, room temperature
- ¾ cups whole milk
- 1 cup lager style beer
- ½ cup oil (canola, vegetable or coconut oil)
- 1 tsp vanilla
- 1 cup crumbled, cooked bacon

Directions

1. Whisk together the eggs, whole milk, beer, oil and vanilla extract.

2. Combine all your ingredients and break up the eggs.

3. Add all of the dry ingredients, except the chocolate chips, to the bowl, whisking constantly to ensure no lumps form in the batter.

4. Stir until a smooth batter forms then let the batter rest for 10 minutes, allowing the batter to thicken. Stir in the bacon.

5. Set your waffle maker to preheat according to the manufacturer's directions. Once the iron is hot, spray with baking spray if needed (some waffle irons are nonstick and therefore do not need spray) then pour the waffle batter into the waffle maker.

6. Cook until golden brown then serve while hot.

7. Cook the remaining waffle batter using the same directions.

Laeken Cucumber

This delicious Laeken Cucumber is a simple delicacy in Belgium.

Serves: 4

Time: 20 minutes

Ingredients

- 1 cucumber cut in half lengthwise
- cold salmon, 12 oz.
- whipped cream, 3 tbsp
- chives, for garnish

Directions

1. Cut the cucumber halves into 5 segments. Scoop out the inside of the cucumber.

2. Add some of the salmon to each piece, then top with whipped cream and some snipped chives.

Peanut Butter Waffles

Not only are these waffles very flavorful but they are also a great way to add a little plant based protein into your breakfast routine.

Serves: 6

Time: 15 minutes

Ingredients

- 2 cups white flour
- 1 tbsp granulated sugar
- 1 1/3 tbsp baking powder
- 1 pinch sea salt
- 2 large eggs, room temperature
- 1 ¾ cups whole milk
- ½ cup oil (canola, vegetable or coconut oil)
- 1 tsp vanilla
- ½ cup smooth peanut butter

Directions

1. Whisk together the eggs, whole milk, oil and vanilla extract. Combine all your ingredients and break up the eggs.

2. Add the peanut butter to the mix, stirring until well combined.

3. Add in all your dry ingredients to the bowl, whisking constantly to ensure no lumps form in the batter.

1. Stir until a smooth batter forms then let the batter rest for 10 minutes, allowing the batter to thicken.

4. Set your waffle maker to preheat according to the manufacturer's directions. Once the iron is hot, spray with baking spray if needed then pour the waffle batter into the waffle maker.

5. Cook until golden brown then serve while hot. Cook the remaining waffle batter using the same directions.

Tomates-Crevette

This tasty shrimp dish is perfect for picnics and afternoon snacks.

Serves: 4

Time: 20 minutes

Ingredients

- 230g of grey shrimp peeled
- 4 tomatoes
- 5 tablespoons of mayonnaise
- lemon juice
- parsley leaves finely chopped
- salt, to taste
- black pepper, to taste

Directions

1. Cut the top off the tomatoes. Excavate the inside. Put them upside down on a plate for 10 minutes.

2. Mix the mayonnaise and lemon juice together. Add the parsley. and mix. Add in your shrimp, some salt and pepper and toss.

3. Put this mix inside the tomatoes, put the top of the tomatoes back on and cool in the refrigerator before serving.

Churro Waffles

Churros are a classic cinnamon and sugar treat that are typically made by frying dough then tossing it in cinnamon and sugar. Now you can enjoy the same flavors in a waffle.

Time: 20 minutes

Serves: 6

Ingredients

- 2 cups white flour
- 1 tbsp granulated sugar
- 1 tsp ground cinnamon
- 1 1/3 tbsp baking powder
- 1 pinch sea salt
- 2 large eggs, room temperature
- 1 ¾ cups whole milk
- ½ cup oil (canola)
- 1 tsp vanilla
- ¼ cup sugar
- 1 tsp ground cinnamon

Directions

1. In a small bowl, combine the ¼ cup sugar and 1 tsp ground cinnamon and stir together. Set aside.

2. Whisk together the eggs, whole milk, oil and vanilla extract. Combine all of your ingredients and break up the eggs.

3. Add all of the dry ingredients, using just the 1 tbsp sugar and 1 tsp of the cinnamon, to the bowl, whisking constantly to ensure no lumps form in the batter.

4. Stir until a smooth batter forms then let the batter rest for 10 minutes, allowing the batter to thicken.

5. Set your waffle maker to preheat.

6. Once the iron is hot, spray with baking spray if needed (some waffle irons are nonstick and therefore do not need spray) then pour the waffle batter into the waffle maker.

7. Cook until golden brown then toss in the cinnamon sugar mix while they are hot.

8. Serve while hot and cook the remaining waffle batter using the same directions.

Creamed Cabbage

In Belgium cuisine, creamed cabbage is a delicious dish that can be enjoyed at any day of the week.

Serves: 4

Time: 20 minutes

Ingredients

- 1 cabbage with core and outer leaves removed, and cut into small pieces
- 1 cup/250ml of cream
- 3 tablespoons of butter
- 1 pinch nutmeg
- Salt, to taste
- black pepper, to taste

Directions

1. Add in your cabbage in a pot of boiling salted water. Cook for 3 minutes.

2. Drain the cabbage, then put it in a baked baking dish, then add the cream and some pepper, 1 pinch nutmeg and salt.

3. Cook in a 350F preheated oven for 15 minutes.

Milk Soup

Spin your carton of milk into a bowl of delicious, creamy soup with this Milk Soup recipe.

Serves: 4

Time: 45 minutes

Ingredients

- 3 chopped leeks
- 1 chopped onion
- 2 peeled and chopped potatoes
- 2 chopped endive leaves
- 4 cups of milk
- black pepper, to taste
- salt, to taste
- chopped parsley, to garnish
- butter, 1 tbsp.

Directions

1. Cook the leeks, endive, and onion in the butter for 10 minutes on a medium heat.

2. Add the potatoes, milk and some salt and pepper. Cover and cook on a low heat for 30 minutes.

3. Serve with some parsley sprinkled on top.

Bacon Cheddar Waffles

No need to choose between breakfast ideas anymore when they are all combined into one perfect waffle recipe.

Serves: 8

Time: 15 minutes

Ingredients

- 2 cups white flour
- 1 tsp granulated sugar
- 1 1/3 tbsp baking powder
- 1 pinch sea salt
- 2 large eggs, room temperature
- 1 ¾ cups whole milk
- ½ cup oil (canola, vegetable or coconut oil)
- ½ cup shredded cheddar cheese
- ½ cup crumbled, cooked bacon

Directions

1. Whisk together the eggs, whole milk, oil and pesto. Combine all of your ingredients and break up the eggs.

2. Add in all your dry ingredients to the bowl, whisking constantly to ensure no lumps form in the batter.

3. Stir until a smooth batter forms then let the batter rest for 10 minutes, allowing the batter to thicken.

4. Fold in the shredded cheese and bacon crumbles. Set your waffle maker to preheat according to the manufacturer's directions.

5. Once the iron is hot, spray with baking spray if needed then pour the waffle batter into the waffle maker.

6. Cook until golden brown then serve while hot.

7. Cook the remaining waffle batter using the same directions.

Cod with Beer Sauce

Beer greatly compliments seafood as it does in this tasty od with Beer Sauce recipe.

Serves: 4

Time: 45 minutes

Ingredients

- 18 oz of cod fillets
- 1 peeled and chopped onion
- 1 cup of cream
- 1 cup of pale ale beer
- chopped chervil

Directions:

1. Butter a baking dish. Add the cod to it.

2. Mix the beer, cream, onion and some salt and pepper. Pout into the baking dish.

3. Cook for 30 minutes in a preheated oven at 180c.

4. Serve with chopped chervil on top.

Peanut Butter Chocolate Chip Waffles

Need a waffle recipe that is filling, decadent and also easy to make.

Serves: 6

Time: 15 minutes

Ingredients

- 2 cups white flour
- 1 tbsp granulated sugar
- 1 1/3 tbsp baking powder
- 1 pinch sea salt
- 2 large eggs, room temperature
- 1 ¾ cups whole milk
- ½ cup oil (canola, vegetable or coconut oil)
- 1 tsp vanilla
- ½ cup smooth peanut butter
- ½ cup mini chocolate chips

Directions

1. Whisk together the eggs, whole milk, oil and vanilla extract.

2. Combine all of your ingredients and break up the eggs.

3. Add the peanut butter to the mix, stirring until well combined.

4. Add in all of your dry ingredients to the bowl, whisking constantly to ensure no lumps form in the batter.

5. Stir until a smooth batter forms then let the batter rest for 10 minutes, allowing the batter to thicken.

6. Gently fold in the chocolate chips.

7. Set your waffle maker to preheat according to the manufacturer's directions. Once the iron is hot, spray with baking spray if needed then pour the waffle batter into the waffle maker.

8. Cook until golden brown then serve while hot.

9. Cook the remaining waffle batter using the same directions.

Baked Skate

Allow this delicious Skate dish to change your lunch and dinner routine for the better.

Serves: 4

Time: 45 minutes

Ingredients

- 4 skate fillets
- half a pint of dark beer/240ml
- a quarter of a pint/120ml of vinegar
- 1 teaspoon of mixed spice
- some dried mixed herbs
- chopped parsley, for garnish
- butter, 2 tbsp.
- black pepper, to taste
- salt, to taste

Directions

1. Butter a baking dish. Season the skate with salt, pepper, parsley and mixed spice.

2. Add the skate fillets to the baking dish. Mix the beer and vinegar with some dried herbs and pour the mix over the fish. Season with a little salt.

3. Put a piece of buttered greaseproof paper over the fish and bake in a moderate oven for one hour.

Cheesy Waffles

Waffles are the perfect savory food and these cheesy waffles are a great example.

Time: 15 minutes

Serve: 6 servings

Ingredients

- 2 cups white flour
- 1 tsp granulated sugar
- 1 1/3 tbsp baking powder
- 1 pinch sea salt
- 2 large eggs, room temperature
- 1 ¾ cups whole milk
- ½ cup oil (canola, vegetable or coconut oil)
- 1 cup shredded cheddar cheese

Directions

1. Whisk together the eggs, whole milk, oil and pesto. Combine all your ingredients and break up the eggs.

2. Add in all your dry ingredients to the bowl, whisking constantly to ensure no lumps form in the batter.

3. Stir until a smooth batter forms then let the batter rest for 10 minutes, allowing the batter to thicken.

4. Fold in the shredded cheddar cheese. Set your waffle maker to preheat according to the manufacturer's directions.

5. Once the iron is hot, spray with baking spray if needed then pour the waffle batter into the waffle maker.

6. Cook until golden brown then serve while hot.

7. Cook the remaining waffle batter using the same directions.

Celery with Bacon

This Celery with Bacon recipe adds a smokey aroma to your celery that you won't be able to deny.

Serves: 4

Time: 15 minutes

Ingredients

- 450g of celery with tops removed and chopped into pieces
- 230g of potatoes peeled and sliced
- 6 slices of bacon
- Vinegar, as needed

Directions

1. Put the celery in boiling salted water. Simmer for 5 minutes. Add the potatoes and cook until the potatoes are cooked. Drain and place on a plate.

2. Fry the bacon.

3. Arrange the celery and potato slices on a plate. Sprinkle over some of the bacon fat from the pan and a little vinegar. Put the bacon rasher on top.

Pesto Waffles

These waffles are savory and slightly sweet while also being full of pesto flavor.

Serve: 6

Time: 15 minutes

Ingredients

- 2 cups white flour
- 1 tsp granulated sugar
- 1 1/3 tbsp baking powder
- 1 pinch sea salt
- 2 large eggs, room temperature
- 1 ¾ cups whole milk
- ½ cup oil (canola, vegetable or coconut oil)
- ½ cup pesto

Directions

1. Whisk together the eggs, whole milk, oil and pesto. Combine all your ingredients and break up the eggs.

2. Add in your dry ingredients to the bowl, whisking constantly to ensure no lumps form in the batter.

3. Stir until a smooth batter forms then let the batter rest for 10 minutes, allowing the batter to thicken.

4. Fold in the crushed Oreo pieces

5. Set your waffle maker to preheat according to the manufacturer's directions. Once the iron is hot, spray with baking spray if needed then pour the waffle batter into the waffle maker.

6. Cook until golden brown then serve while hot.

7. Cook the remaining waffle batter using the same directions.

Flemish Sauce

This Flemish Sauce gives you a simple sauce for any seafood dish.

Serves: 4

Time: 7 minutes

Ingredients

- 1 tablespoon of flour
- 1 tablespoon of water
- 3 egg yolks
- 230g of butter
- juice from half a lemon
- 1 pinch nutmeg
- Salt, to taste

Directions

1. Melt the butter.

2. Set a glass bowl on a pan of hot water on a warm heat. Add the flour and water to the bowl, mix and boil for 4 minutes.

3. Whisk in the egg yolks, butter, some 1 pinch nutmeg and lemon juice.

4. Serve with fish.

Chicken and Waffles

This recipe combines two iconic foods into one easy to follow.

Serves: 8

Time: 15 minutes

Ingredients

- 2 cups white flour

- 1 tbsp granulated sugar

- 1 1/3 tbsp baking powder

- 1 pinch sea salt

- 2 large eggs, room temperature

- 1 ¾ cups whole milk

- ½ cup oil (canola, vegetable or coconut oil)

- 1 cup shredded rotisserie chicken, cooked

Directions

1. Whisk together the eggs, whole milk, oil and vanilla extract.

2. Combine all your ingredients and break up the eggs.

3. Add in all your dry ingredients to the bowl, whisking constantly to ensure no lumps form in the batter.

4. Stir until a smooth batter forms then let the batter rest for 10 minutes, allowing the batter to thicken.

5. Fold in the shredded rotisserie chicken.

6. Set your waffle maker to preheat according to the manufacturer's directions. Once the iron is hot, spray with baking spray if needed then pour the waffle batter into the waffle maker.

7. Cook until golden brown then serve while hot.

8. Cook the remaining waffle batter using the same directions.

Fricadell

This delicious meatloaf sandwich makes for a heavy lunch on its own or dinner paired with a salad.

Serves: 4

Time: 7 minutes

Ingredients

- 680g of minced pork
- three slices of bread
- two eggs
- salt, to taste
- pepper, to taste

Directions

1. Mix the meat, eggs and salt and pepper.

2. Put in a baking dish and bake in a medium hot oven for 30 minutes.

3. Slice and use to form sandwiches then serve with a salad.

Apple Spice Waffles

These waffles are soft, moist and full of delicious fall flavors.

Serves: 6

Time: 20 minutes

Ingredients

- 2 cups white flour
- 1 tbsp granulated sugar
- 1 tsp cinnamon
- ¼ tsp 1 pinch nutmeg
- 1 1/3 tbsp baking powder
- 1 pinch sea salt
- 2 large eggs, room temperature
- ½ cup grated apple
- 1 cup whole milk
- ½ cup oil (canola, vegetable or coconut oil)
- 1 tsp vanilla

Directions

1. Whisk together the eggs, whole milk, oil and vanilla extract. Combine all of your ingredients and break up the eggs.

2. Stir in the grated apples.

3. Add in all your dry ingredients to the bowl, whisking constantly to ensure no lumps form in the batter. Stir until a smooth batter forms then let the batter rest for 10 minutes, allowing the batter to thicken.

4. Set your waffle maker to preheat according to the manufacturer's directions. Once the iron is hot, spray with baking spray if needed then cook until golden.

5. Serve while hot. Cook the remaining waffle batter using the same directions.

Conclusion

Belgium cuisine is filled with dishes to provide fun, frolic and family gatherings. I sincerely hope that these 30 deliciously simple Belgium recipes. Practice makes perfect, so please continue cooking your favorite recipes as many times as you like. Then share them with your friends and family.

If you enjoyed what you read through, please take a few minutes to leave a review on the store on which you purchased the book.

Happy Cooking!

About the Author

Born in New Germantown, Pennsylvania, Stephanie Sharp received a Masters degree from Penn State in English Literature. Driven by her passion to create culinary masterpieces, she applied and was accepted to The International Culinary School of the Art Institute where she excelled in French cuisine. She has married her cooking skills with an aptitude for business by opening her own small cooking school where she teaches students of all ages.

Stephanie's talents extend to being an author as well and she has written over 400 e-books on the art of cooking and baking that include her most popular recipes.

Sharp has been fortunate enough to raise a family near her hometown in Pennsylvania where she, her husband and children live in a beautiful rustic house on an extensive piece of land. Her other passion is taking care of the furry members of her family which include 3 cats, 2 dogs and a potbelly pig named Wilbur.

Watch for more amazing books by Stephanie Sharp coming out in the next few months.

Author's Afterthoughts

I am truly grateful to you for taking the time to read my book. I cherish all of my readers! Thanks ever so much to each of my cherished readers for investing the time to read this book!

With so many options available to you, your choice to buy my book is an honour, so my heartfelt thanks at reading it from beginning to end!

I value your feedback, so please take a moment to submit an honest and open review on Amazon so I can get valuable insight into my readers' opinions and others can benefit from your experience.

Thank you for taking the time to review!

Stephanie Sharp

For announcements about new releases, please

follow my author page on Amazon.com!

You can find that at:

https://www.amazon.com/author/stephanie-sharp

*or Scan **QR-code** below.*